# Pressing
# RESET
## for
# Healthy
# Shoulders

original
**strength**

Copyright © 2020 Original Strength Systems, LLC

ALL RIGHTS RESERVED. This book contains material protected under International and Federal Copyright Laws and Treaties. Any unauthorized reprint or use of this material is prohibited. No part of this book may be reproduced or transmitted in any form or by any means, electronic or mechanical, including photocopying, recording, or by any information storage and retrieval system without express written permission from the author/publisher.

Nicole Clark, PT, DPT, SCS, ITPT, OS Certified Clinician - nicoleclark12@gmail.com
Mark Shropshire, MS - www.markshropshire.com

ISBN: 978-1-64184-278-5 (Paperback)

Your shoulders are awesome! From the mundane aspects of everyday life - helping you brush your teeth, combing your hair, and driving you to work to some seriously cool things - throwing a baseball at 95 mph, pressing hundreds of pounds of weight, swimming in triathlons, and climbing mountains. Truly, shoulders allow us to live full and enriched lives.

Except when they hurt!!

When that happens, stuff like getting dressed or getting up off the ground can seem impossible. If this is you, or if you have shoulders and don't want it to become you - listen up! There is a simple and easy way for you to keep your shoulders healthy and strong throughout the rest of your life - the way you were designed. It requires zero athletic expertise, zero equipment, and fewer than 10 - 15 minutes. Sounds good, right?!

The "it" in this case is a movement restoration program known as Original Strength. What's the deal with the name? Well, we mean that you can regain or improve your movement and strength now the same way you "originally" did when you were a child. Think about it - we all figured out how to get around and move on our own without coaches or special programs to follow. Doctors call this process the Neuro-Developmental Movement Sequence. Original Strength takes us back to these same movements that we all once used and helps us to rewire or reset our body's nervous systems. It's the process of resetting the nervous system that allows us to move better. In a general sense this can mean our bodies feel better. But specific to this manual, we are talking shoulders!

## Here is how it works:

Original Strength follows the three pillars of human movement:

1. Diaphragmatic Breathing
2. Activation of the Vestibular System - (helps with balance and sensory information processing)
3. Perform Contralateral or Midline Crossing Movements (reaching across the body or moving limbs on opposite sides of the body)

These three pillars are already programmed into our nervous system when we are born and are the basis for human movement. As we grow, we naturally utilize the pillars to become stronger and to learn how to move and interact with the world. It's essential to continue to use these throughout our lifespan to keep our nervous system and body healthy and strong. By establishing our original strength, we have the opportunity to engage in life fully. Here's the simple on how to Press RESET on our bodies and get our shoulders working optimally:

1. Diaphragmatic Breathing aka Belly Breathing
2. Eye/Head Control
3. Rolling

4. Rocking
5. Crawling/Contralateral Movements

If you are asking yourself how does breathing or any of this stuff relate to my shoulders, you are probably not alone. Patience dear reader…..so before we get too carried away with all this – please understand the following:

Medical Disclaimer – We are not here to treat, diagnose, or prescribe for any physical condition. It's important to note that this is a guide for those looking for healthy, happy shoulders. This does not trump that of medical advice for your doctor or a professional. If at any time you experience pain when following this guide, STOP. DON'T MOVE INTO PAIN – pain changes how you move. A regression may be required. We are only here to show how the human body was designed to move. In the process of moving correctly, good things can happen. However, it would also be advised to seek advice from a medical professional if you are having pain.

Having said that, here is how OS (Original Strength is a lot to type so let's just go with OS, OK?) helps your shoulders feel, move and perform better

A little background will help……during our development as children, the shoulder learned how to function and stabilize reflexively, all on its own. It learned how to do its job and work with other parts of the body to create movement. This is important for all types of movements, whether in sports, fitness training, or just daily life. Movement is movement – it doesn't really matter what the arena is.

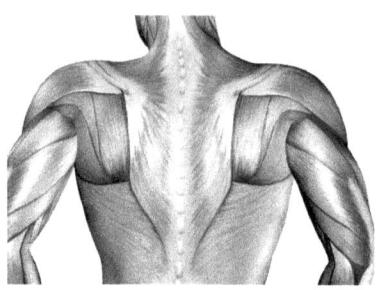

Now, the good stuff: If you want healthy shoulders, a good place to start is the spine. Here is why. The shoulder is anchored to the bones of the spine via muscle-tendon connections, which then connect to the scapula or, as it's better known - the shoulder blade. All of these structures and the muscles attached to them have to work in concert with one another for the shoulder joint to work up to its potential.

When the spine has optimal levels of mobility and stability, that allows for optimal functioning of the scapula (shoulder blade) and the muscles that attach to it (see the "posterior view" picture below) In turn, this set up allows for optimal functioning of the glenohumeral joint (shoulder). All of this indicates that movement efficiency at the spine will lead to movement efficiency at the scapula, which in turn leads to movement efficiency at the shoulder joint.

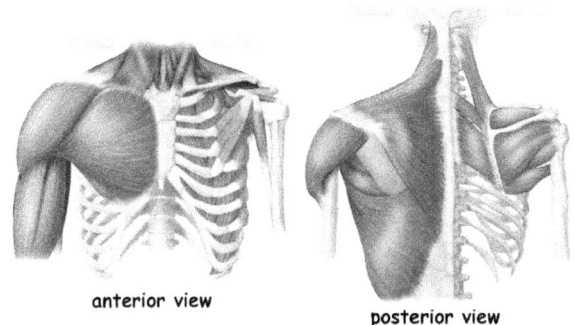

anterior view    posterior view

An overly stiff spine (too stable – lacking enough mobility) can result in dysfunction of the muscles attaching to both the spine and the scapula, leading to poor scapular movement. This can result in the shoulder not working in the way it was designed to. Because of this dysfunction, movement compensations typically occur. Over time, these compensations become our "normal way" of doing things and can lead to poor shoulder health and possibly pain. This is where Pressing RESET for the shoulder comes in... Let's get started!!

Some pieces of information are so important, they are worth restating. We call this type of information a PEARL. You will see PEARL throughout the booklet. Please look for them.

# Pressing
# RESET

## Reset #1

# Diaphragmatic Breathing

## Why?

- The diaphragm is a primary stabilizer of the spine, helping it to function correctly.
- It is our primary respiratory muscle
  - » When we don't use the diaphragm for breathing, we compensate with other muscles of the neck and upper body using them for a job that they are not designed for. This causes them to feel tight, stiff, and overworked.
- Breathing using the diaphragm stimulates the parasympathetic nervous system. One of the many benefits of activating this part of the nervous system is that it reduces muscular tension in the body. This helps you relax and begin the process of resetting your nervous system to control your body the way it was designed to be used.
- When the diaphragm does its job, the movement of that muscle helps to gently mobilize the thoracic spine for improved spinal mobility.

- » This part of the spine is where many of the muscles that attach the shoulder blade to the spine are located.

## How?

- Mouth closed and tongue on the roof of the mouth.
    - » PEARL – Frees up the neck's full range of motion.
- Slowly breathe in and out of your nose, pulling air into your belly.
- When you inhale, your belly should expand. When you exhale it should deflate. Try not to let your upper chest and shoulders heave when you breathe!

# Position 1
SUPINE

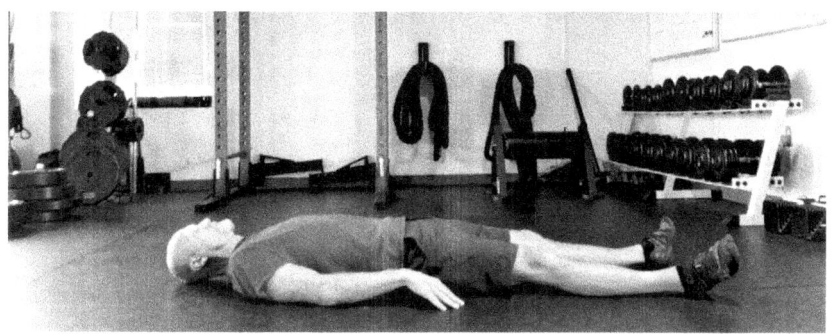

# Position 2
PRONE

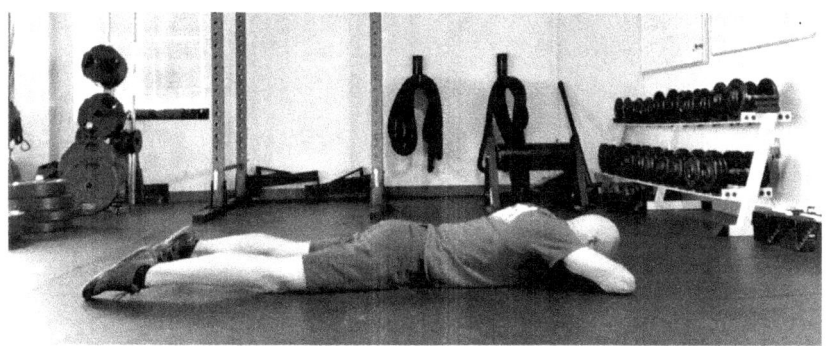

## Reset #2
# Eye/Head Control

## Why?

- Movement of the head mobilizes the entire spine but especially the cervical and thoracic spine (upper and mid-spine).
    - » These areas are also anchor points for muscles that influence the shoulder blade and, therefore, the shoulder joint. Consequently, optimizing both the stability and mobility of the head and neck will contribute to optimal shoulder health.
    - » PEARL – Movement of the head and spine nourishes the spine with all kinds of useful sensory information. If you haven't done this in a while, your spine will love it!
    - » PEARL – Movement of the head stimulates your vestibular system. This is essential for the reflexive management of posture and balance.

# How?

# Laying on your back:

## Movement 1
CHIN TUCKS

- Lay on your back.
- Mouth closed with tongue on the roof of the mouth.
- Eyes lead the head – so look down first, then move the head.
- Don't hold your breath.

# Movement 2

## SUPINE CHIN TUCK + NECK FLEXION
(LOOK DOWN AT YOUR CHEST)

- Lay on your back.
- Mouth closed with tongue on the roof of the mouth.
- Lead with the eyes.
- Then tuck your chin to your sternum and lift your head off the floor as much as you are able to do without pain.
- Don't hold your breath.

# Prone on your elbows:

## Movement 3
### HEAD NODS

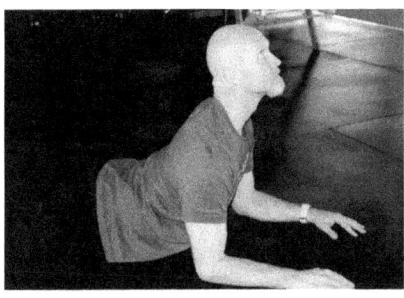 

- Lay on your stomach - support yourself on your elbows.
- Keep your chest up as high as you comfortably can.
- Mouth closed with tongue on the roof of the mouth.
- Lead with the eyes.
- Move your head up and down as much as you can without pain!
- Don't hold your breath.
  - » If the floor is not something you can get to, seated head nods will work too!

# Movement 4

HEAD ROTATIONS

- Lay on your stomach – Support yourself on your elbows.
- Mouth closed with tongue on the roof of the mouth.
- Lead with the eyes.
- Turn the head to the side, looking over (not around) your shoulder.
- Allow the shoulders to move out of the way as you move your head.
    - » You might even feel your shoulder blade sliding down your rib cage when you do this – cool!

# Movement 5

QUADRUPED

- Try the same movements in quadruped if that is a more comfortable position for you.

# Reset #3
# Rolling

## Why?

- Neurologically connects the shoulder to the opposite hip.
  » The hips and shoulders naturally work together – think walking, running or throwing for example.
- Rolling nourishes the entire spine with movement in a safe and feel-good way.
- Rolling crosses the midline of the body. Whenever we do things like this, it links the two hemispheres of the brain together.
  » This is important for coordinated movement, synchronizing fine and gross motor skills, cognitive tasks such as reading and writing, and even maintaining attention and concentration!
- Rolling reflexively retrains stabilization of the spine, so the spine is stabilized before arm movement.
  » The spine needs to be stable before your scapula and arm move. This translates to safer movement, and increased force output of the shoulder joint.

# How?

## Movement 1
EGG ROLLS

- Mouth closed with tongue on the roof of the mouth.
- Lead with eyes, then the head.
- Laying on your back, tuck knees to chest and hold onto each knee with one hand.
- Look first, then rotate the head to the side and let the body follow so you are lying on your side tucked into a ball.
  - » Turn the head as far as you safely can once you are on your side to fully rotate the head and spine.
- Rotate your head to the opposite shoulder and once again let the body follow, so you are lying on your other side.
  - » Be sure to move the eyes and the head – the rest of the body plays catch up.

# Movement 2

WIPERS

- Mouth closed with tongue on the roof of the mouth.
- Lie on your back and place your arms perpendicular to your torso.
- Bend your knees up toward your chest to lift your tailbone off the floor. Your feet will be in the air.
- While keeping your shoulder blades in contact with the ground, rotate your legs from side to side.
- Keep your knees pulled up toward your chest even as you rotate your legs to the side. Do not let them drift away.

# Movement 3

## UPPER BODY HALF ROLLS

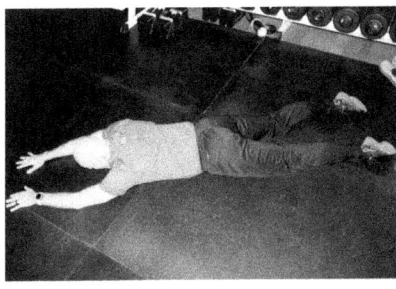 

- Belly to back
    - » Mouth closed with tongue on the roof of the mouth.
    - » Lie on your belly with your arms overhead.
    - » Bend your right elbow, look at it, and reach for the floor behind you. Try to touch the floor with your elbow.
    - » Then, roll back to your belly.
    - » Do the same thing on the left side.
    - » Keep your lower body relaxed, almost limp throughout the movement.

# Movement 4

## LOWER BODY HALF ROLLS

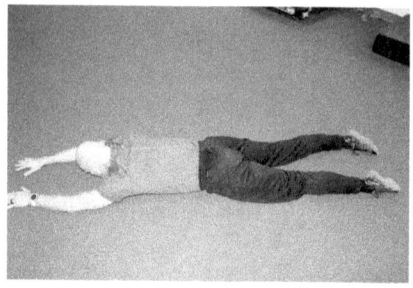
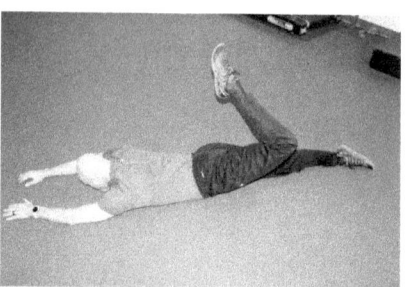
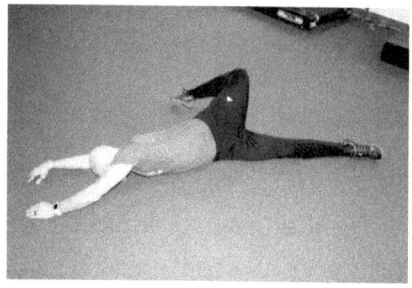

- » Mouth closed with tongue on the roof of the mouth.
- » Lie on your belly with your arms overhead.
- » Bend your right knee and lift it off the floor. Reach your foot across the midline of the body to the other side.
- » Then roll back to your belly.
- » Repeat on the other side.
- » Keep your upper body loose and relaxed throughout the movement.

# Movement 5

NECK AND SHOULDER ROLL

- Mouth closed with tongue on the roof of the mouth.
- Lie on your back with your left knee up, foot on the floor.
- Look to the right and up, like you are trying to see behind yourself.
- Reach across the body with your left arm and at the same time bridge your hips off the floor.
  - » The weight of the body should be on the shoulder, not the head or neck.
- Keep reaching across yourself until your body naturally rolls over on to your belly.
- Roll back on to your back any way that you would like and repeat for the other side.

# Movement 6

ALL 4's ROLL

- Mouth closed, with tongue on the roof of the mouth.
- Start on your hands and knees (quadruped position) with your head up on the horizon if you can.
- Lift one leg off the ground, keeping the knee bent. Reaching with the foot, cross the midline of the body and set the foot down on the floor.
- As you do the above, allow the same side hand to come off the ground, but only when you have to (when you can't twist your body any more!).
- Look up and reach your hand to the sky, keeping your knees as far apart as you can.
- Then, look at the floor and reach your hand down just past your face, to the floor (it should feel like you are uncoiling).
- When you need to, release the foot from the floor and return it to the starting position.

## Reset #4

## Rocking

## Why?

- Rocking is actually reflexive strength training for the shoulder! This is one of the ways you developed the strength and stability of your shoulders to begin with!
  » Rocking forward is really transferring your body weight from your feet to your hands. This causes compression of the joints in your arm (wrist, elbow, and shoulder).
  » These forces are detected by your nervous system. To keep you from falling on your face and hurting yourself, it quickly turns on the stabilizers of the shoulders, shoulder blades, and your spine (you might even feel this in your core!)
  » When you do a lot of rocking, it improves and speeds up the reflexive timing and activation of the shoulder complex and improves motor control.
  » Keeps the spine healthy as rocking with the head held up improves the posture of the spine.
- Further strengthens the connection of the shoulder to the hip.

- Rocking helps to integrate the shoulders into the rest of the body.
  - » PEARL – Rocking is very soothing to the nervous system and helps to calm the body naturally.

# How?

## Movement 1
QUADRUPED ROCKING

- Get on your hands and knees to start.
- Mouth closed with tongue on the roof of the mouth.
- Your eyes and head should be held up with your eyes on the horizon.
- Think "big chest" and hold your sternum up high.
- Rock back and forth, shifting your weight from your toes to your hands, then back to your feet again.
- Keep your back flat, and don't let it round / bow up when you are moving.

# Movement 2

## COMMANDO ROCKING

- Get on your forearms and knees to start.
- Mouth closed with tongue on the roof of the mouth.
- Your eyes and head should be held up with your eyes on the horizon.
- Think "big chest" and hold your sternum up high.
- Rock back and forth, shifting your weight from your toes to your forearms, then back to your feet again.
- Keep your back flat, and don't let it round / bow up when you are moving.

# Movement 3

SINGLE ARM AND LEG ROCKING

- Mouth closed with tongue on the roof of the mouth.
- Lift one of your arms and your opposite leg off the ground, so they point in opposing directions.
- Simply rock forward and back. When you need to place your hand on the ground, do so. Same goes for the foot as you rock backwards.

# Movement 4

LATERAL ROCKING

- Mouth closed with tongue on the roof of the mouth.
- Keep your head up on the horizon as best you can.
- Simply shift your weight from side to side (hand to hand) as far as you comfortably can, crossing midline in the process.
- Don't forget to breathe through your nose, and don't hold your breath!

# Movement 5

ROCK IN A CIRCLE

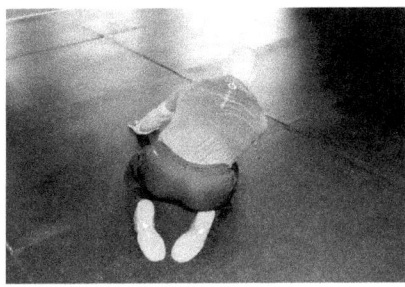 

- Mouth closed with tongue on the roof of the mouth.
- Keep your head up on the horizon as best you can.
- As you rock forward, shift your weight in a circular fashion moving from one hand to the other, and one knee to the other as you rock back towards your heels.
- Don't forget to breathe through your nose, and don't hold your breath!

## Reset #5

# Crawling/Contralateral Movements

## Why?

- Further strengthens the connection between the shoulder and hip.
  - » As you crawl, the demand placed on the entire body increases. As a result, reflexes are further sharpened, increasing their speed.
- "Higher intensity" strength training for the shoulder.
  - » The shoulder will have to bear the weight of the body alone as you initiate the crawling movement. As a consequence, there is a higher demand placed on the shoulder complex to stabilize and control the movement.
- Crawling helps to establish optimal posture.
- It lays the neurological foundation for all contralateral or cross-lateral limb movements.
  - » PEARL - The more you engage in these patterns, the stronger the patterns become tying you together even further - making your nervous system super-efficient! This makes your shoulders super-efficient as well.

# How?

## Movement 1
HANDS AND KNEES CRAWLING

- Start by getting down on your hands and knees (it's all in the name)
- Mouth closed with the tongue on the roof of the mouth.
- Hold your head up and look at the horizon.
- Keep a "tall" sternum - think big chest.
- Move your opposite arms and legs together and crawl forward or backward.
  - » Keep your knees as wide as your hands if you can.

# Movement 2

## LEOPARD CRAWL

(This is where you make the transition to serious strength training!)

- Start by getting down on your hands and feet.
- Mouth closed with the tongue on the roof of the mouth.
- Hold your head up and look at the horizon.
- Keep a "tall" sternum - think big chest.
- Move your opposite arms and legs together and crawl forward or backward.
- Keep your knees even with and behind your wrists.
- Keep your shins parallel with the ground.

# Contralateral movements without crawling

## Movement 3
SPEED SKATERS

- Get on your hands and knees.
- Mouth closed with the tongue on the roof of the mouth.
- Keep your eyes on the horizon.
- Keep a tall sternum.
- Move your opposite arm and leg back simultaneously. Place them back on the floor and repeat on the opposite side.

# Movement 4

BIRD DOGS

- Get on your hands and knees.
- Mouth closed with tongue on the roof of your mouth.
- Keep your eyes on the horizon.
- Keep a tall sternum.
- Move your opposite arm and leg toward each other, touching your knee to your elbow if you can.
  - » If that is not an option, just touch some part of your arm or hand to your knee!

Your DESIGN

# The Power in Your Design

The power of movement restoration, the hope of healing, and the expression of strength all live in your nervous system. Your very design contains the movement program intended to keep you strong, able, and healthy.

Spending just a few minutes every day, relearning or remembering how to do these movements will enable you to live your life better – with strength and health.

Your body truly is awesomely and wonderfully made. It is designed to be strong and able, always. Everything you need to experience this is inside your nervous system, waiting for you to move with it. In other words, your original strength is inside, it's your move…

# Simple Daily RESET Plan for Healthy Shoulders

So, you may be wondering - how the heck am I supposed to do this stuff now? Should I do all of it every day? Can I get overtrained? How much should I do? Is it OK for kids? Is it OK for older adults?

So many questions!

The simple answer to all of the above is it depends! Not much of an answer, but hear us out on this one. Start where you are. This means everyone has a different starting point. Original Strength, when done correctly, and as outlined in this booklet, is safe for everyone. You can do it every day – just change some of the exercises here and there as you like. Don't think this stuff to death! You'll have your favorites as some of the movements will really feel great, and you'll want to do them every day. Here's a little plan to get you started. Engage in the following at least once a day for the best results.

## Diaphragmatic Breathing

- 3 minutes

## Eye / Head Control

- Supine Chin Tucks + Full Neck Flexion. Hold the tuck for 6 to 8 seconds x 3-5 reps
- Head Nods, prone on your elbows x 20 reps

## Rolling

- Egg Rolls x 10 reps to each side
- Wipers x 20 reps to each side

## Rocking

- Rocking x 3 minutes

## Contralateral Movements / Crawling

- Speed Skaters x 3 min

There you go! Simple, easy, and uncomplicated – kind of like the way life should be, right?

# Want to learn more?

This booklet was designed to give you a brief overview of some of the resets we do in Original Strength and apply them to the specific health of your shoulders. Along the way, you may begin to notice that you feel and move better in general. Feel free to feel good as much as you'd like!

We put it together because we know Pressing RESET can help everyone and anyone. If you do nothing more than what is in this booklet, you will notice many changes in how your body moves and feels. It will benefit both your mind and body!

---

**Original Strength** is a human movement education company with a mission to make the world a better place through movement.

We do this by conducting clinics, courses, training, and certifying coaches and instructors, developing educational materials for PE teachers, physical therapy students, and professionals, as well as many other professions dealing with fitness, health, wellness, sports conditioning, and vestibular and neuromuscular functionality.

If you want to know more about Pressing RESET and regaining your original strength, visit www.originalstrength.net. There you will find a variety of books, free video tutorials (Movement Snax), and a complete listing of our courses, clinics and OS Certified Professionals near you.

You may want to consider finding an OS Certified Professional. These professionals can conduct an Original Strength Screen and Assessment (OSSA), which is the quickest and easiest way to identify areas your movement system needs to go from good to best. The OSSA allows the pro to pinpoint the best place for you and your kids to start Pressing RESET and restoring their original strength.

**Press RESET now and live life better** because you were awesomely and wonderfully made to accomplish amazing things.

For more information:

Original Strength Systems, LLC
OriginalStrength.net

PressingRESETfor@Originalstrength.net